THE OCEAN BLUE AND YOU

Written by
Suzanne Slade

Illustrated by
Stephanie Fizer Coleman

PUBLISHED BY SLEEPING BEAR PRESS™

Drip, drop
raindrops plop.

You're cozy and snug
inside Mama's warm **hug**.

The **sand** beneath you
is soft
and still.

Ocean waves gently **roll** in—

swish

swoosh—

lulling you to sleep.

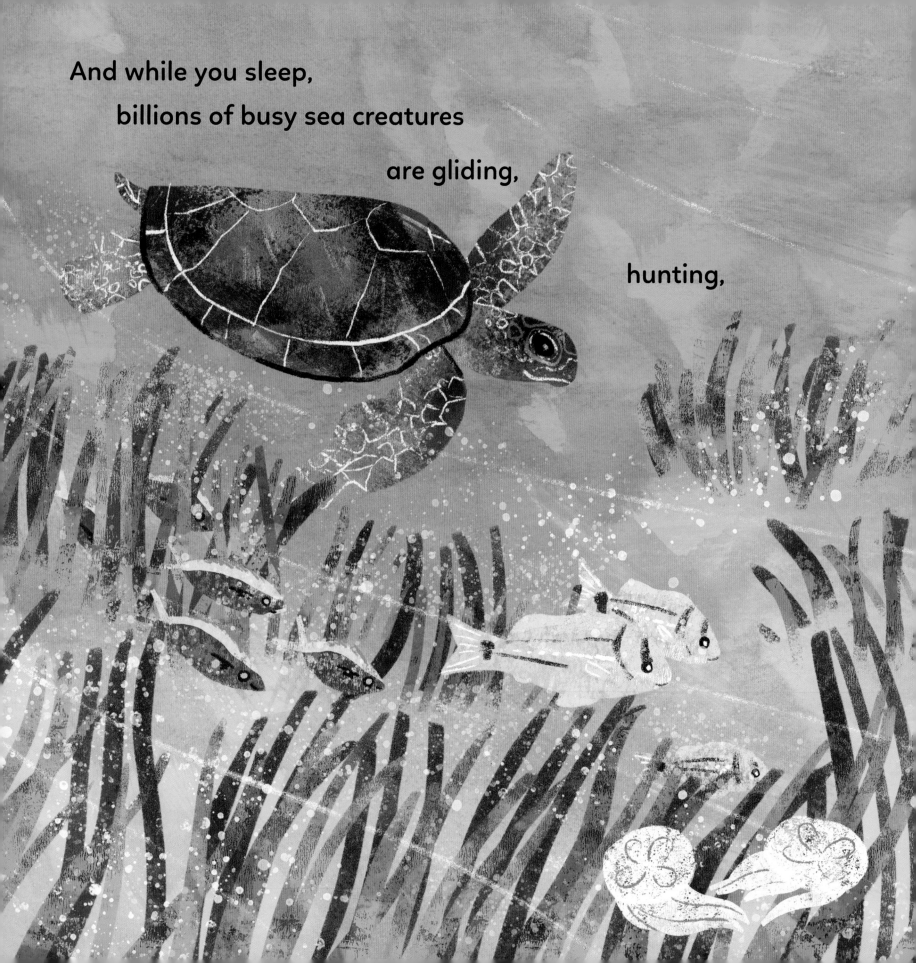

And while you sleep,
billions of busy sea creatures

are gliding,

hunting,

and hiding

in their watery world—
the big **blue ocean**.

The wide, wavy **ocean**

flows across our Earth

from rocky coasts

to tropical rainforests

to sandy beaches

to *you*!
Silently snoozing you.

And while you sleep,
 dreaming big dreams,

hungry sharks,

migrating whales,

and diving dolphins

cruise through salty waters
in the vast **open ocean**.

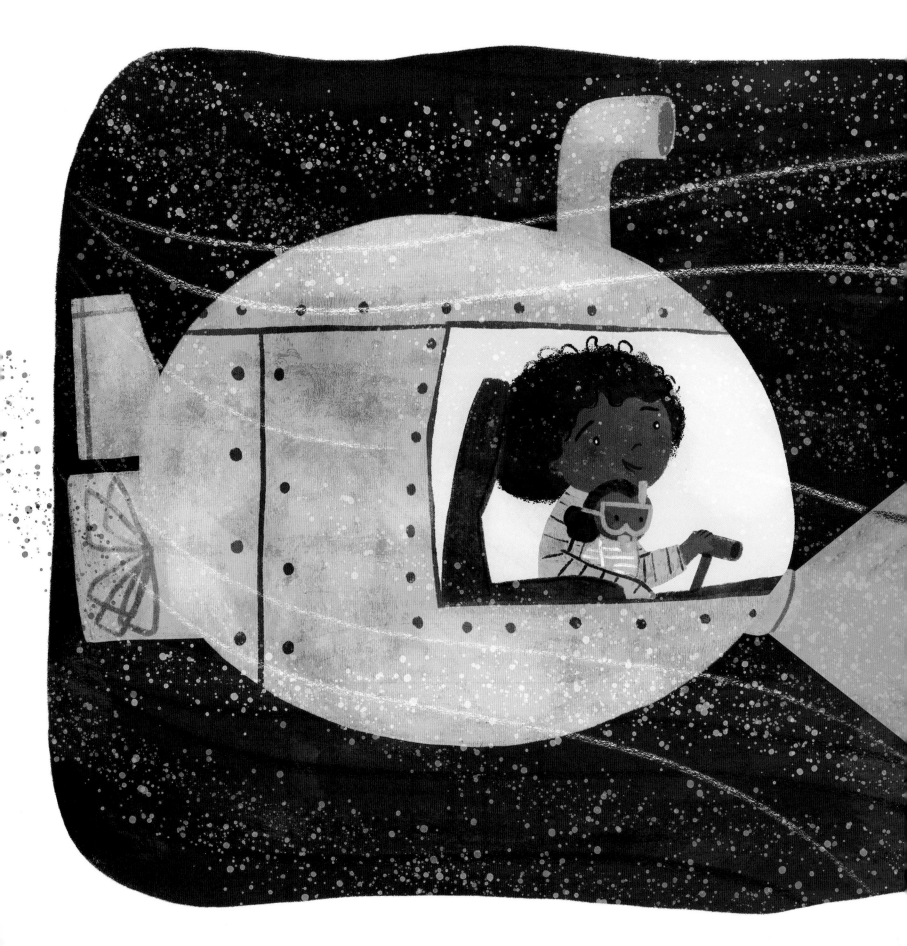

And while you still sleep,
    dreaming even bigger dreams,

schools of brilliant fish

dart past elusive eels

and stealthy stingrays

in their glorious, colorful home—
the **coral reef!**

And then,
slowly but surely—
it happens!

Right on schedule,
the tide slips out to sea
revealing a tiny **tide pool**.

The sun's rays
reach through the **sparkling water**,
sending warm light

to slimy snails,

curious crabs,

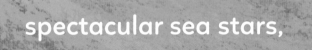

spectacular sea stars,

and *you*!
Silently stirring you.

And when you wake,

all the dolphins in the **open ocean**,

all the stingrays in the **coral reef**,

all the sea stars in the **tide pools,**

are still gliding,
hunting,
and hiding
in our big blue ocean.

Drip, drop.
Raindrops stop.

And you're ready for fun
in the sparkling sun!

Earth is nicknamed the "Blue Planet" due to its massive oceans.

A thick kelp forest provides food and shelter for many animals such as fish, eels, lobsters, and more.

Exploring the Ocean

Earth has five blue oceans—Arctic, Southern, Indian, Atlantic, and Pacific. Together, they hold 95 percent of all the water in the world. From space, Earth looks like a big blue marble because most of its surface is covered with water. Scientists believe only 20 percent of the ocean has been explored.

Our oceans contain different types of habitats. This book shares six: the sea grass meadow, kelp forest, open ocean, deep sea, coral reef, and tide pool. Some ocean habitats, like coral reefs and tide pools, are sunny and warm. Others, such as the deep sea, are dark and cold. Each habitat is a very special place for plants and animals that have adapted, or changed, to survive in that environment.

Though often mistaken for plants, the colorful corals in a coral reef are actually living animals.

This colorful jellyfish, named the Japanese sea nettle, lives in the Pacific Ocean.

Billions of amazing creatures live in the ocean. It is the home of the world's largest animal, the blue whale, which weighs up to 150 tons. The oldest animal species on our planet, such as sponges and jellyfish, also live in the ocean. They've been here for hundreds of millions of years.

Scientists across the globe are studying oceans. Why? Because a healthy ocean means a healthy planet. Oceans provide food for us, contain ingredients for medicines, regulate Earth's temperature, drive the weather (which waters crops), and create about half of our oxygen. The ocean is so important, we need to take good care of it. You can help by using refillable water bottles (reduces plastic litter in oceans), turning off the faucet when you brush your teeth, and taking shorter showers to conserve water. And the next time you visit a beach, pick up litter. If everyone works together, we can protect our oceans!

To Bob and Linda, who love the ocean blue
—Suzanne

★

For Seth

—Stephanie

SLEEPING BEAR PRESS™
2395 South Huron Parkway, Suite 200
Ann Arbor, MI 48104
www.sleepingbearpress.com

Printed and bound in China.

10 9 8 7 6 5 4 3 2 1

Library of Congress Cataloging-in-Publication Data

Names: Slade, Suzanne, author. | Coleman, Stephanie Fizer, illustrator.
Title: The ocean blue and you / written by Suzanne Slade ;
illustrated by Stephanie Fizer Coleman.
Description: Ann Arbor, MI : Sleeping Bear Press, [2024] | Audience: Ages
4-8 years | Summary: "As a child dozes on an oceanside sandy beach, she
dreams of the sea world teeming with life, including the many creatures
and ecosystems found there, from migrating whales to elusive eels to the
colorful coral reefs. Back matter includes science facts"– Provided by publisher.
Identifiers: LCCN 2024005273 | ISBN 9781534112797 (hardcover)
Subjects: LCSH: Ocean–Juvenile literature. | Oceanography–Juvenile literature.
Classification: LCC GC21.5 .S595 2024 | DDC 551.46–dc23/eng/20240323
LC record available at https://lccn.loc.gov/2024005273

Stock Photography: NASA, © Ethan Daniels/Shutterstock.com, © SARAWUT
KUNDEJ/Shutterstock.com, © AlyoshinE/Shutterstock.com.